Nuptse and Lhotse in Nepal

Jocey Asnong

ALL RIGHTS RESERVED. NO PART OF THIS PUBLICATION MAY BE REPRODUCED IN ANY FORM OR BY ANY MEANS WITHOUT THE EXPRESS PRIOR WRITTEN CONSENT OF THE PUBLISHER AND/OR AUTHOR.

Spelling, village names, mountain heights, and other information about Nepal often change between different maps and books.

Nuptse and Lhotse in Nepal/ Written and Illustrated by Jocey Asnong

ISBN 978-9937-0-6141-4

Asnong, Jocelyn, 1973-
Nuptse and Lhotse in Nepal / Written and Illustrated by Jocey Asnong.

ISBN 978-9937-0-6141-4

1. Nepal--Juvenile fiction. 2. Himalaya Mountains--Juvenile fiction.
I. Title.

PS8601.S592N86 2008   jC813'.6   C2008-906012-1

Nepal Edition Published by
Mera Publications Pvt. Ltd
www.merapublications.com

1st Printing 2008 (Canada, 4th Floor Press, Inc.)
2nd Printing 2019 (Nepal, Mera Publications Pvt. Ltd.)

Printed in Nepal

Inner pages printed on 120 gms woodfree paper

www.cautiousleroy.com

**Dedicated
To**
Aven Morgan
May you one day go to the high-up snowy places.

Once upon a time,
a while ago,
maybe sometime last year…

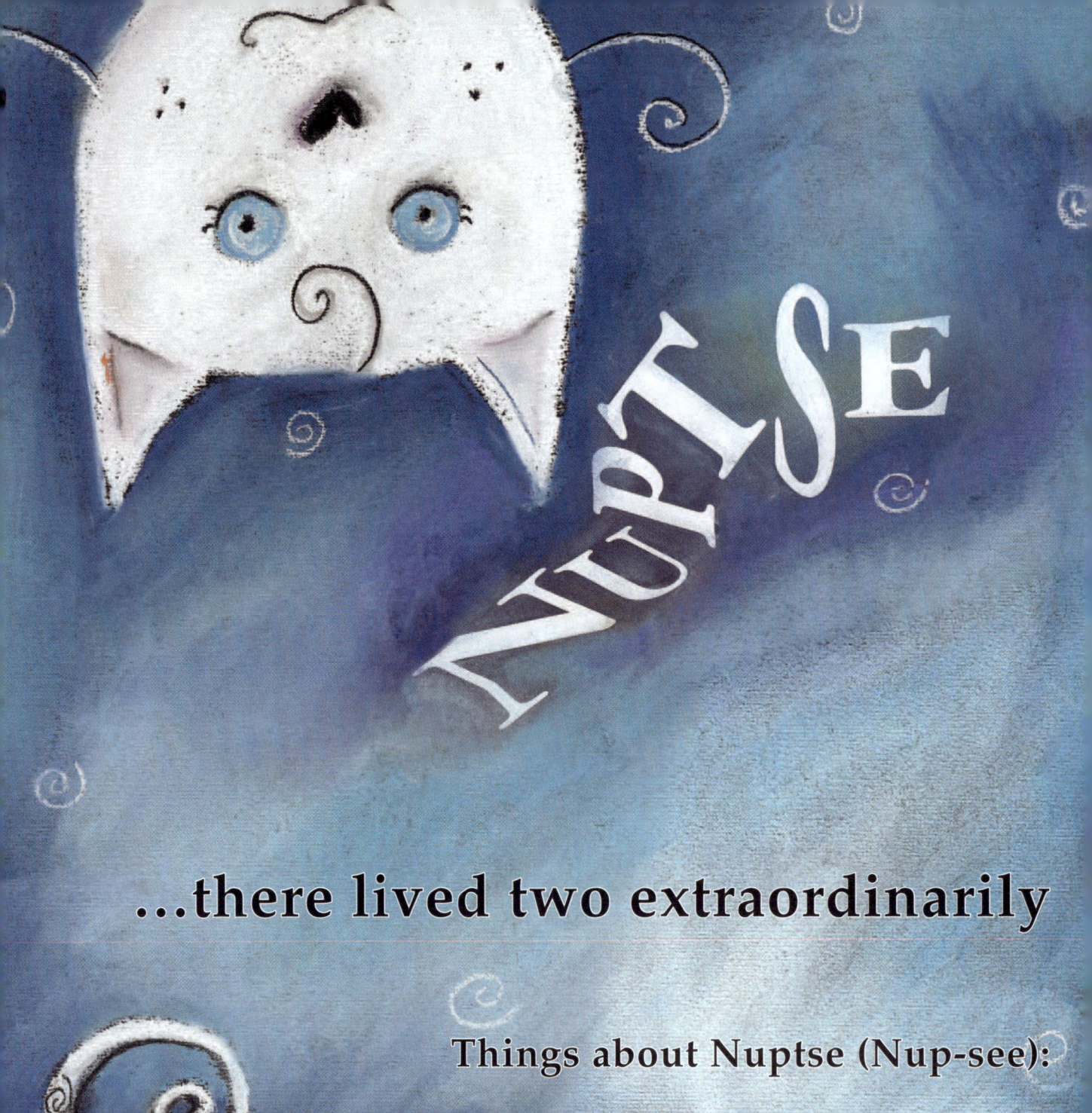

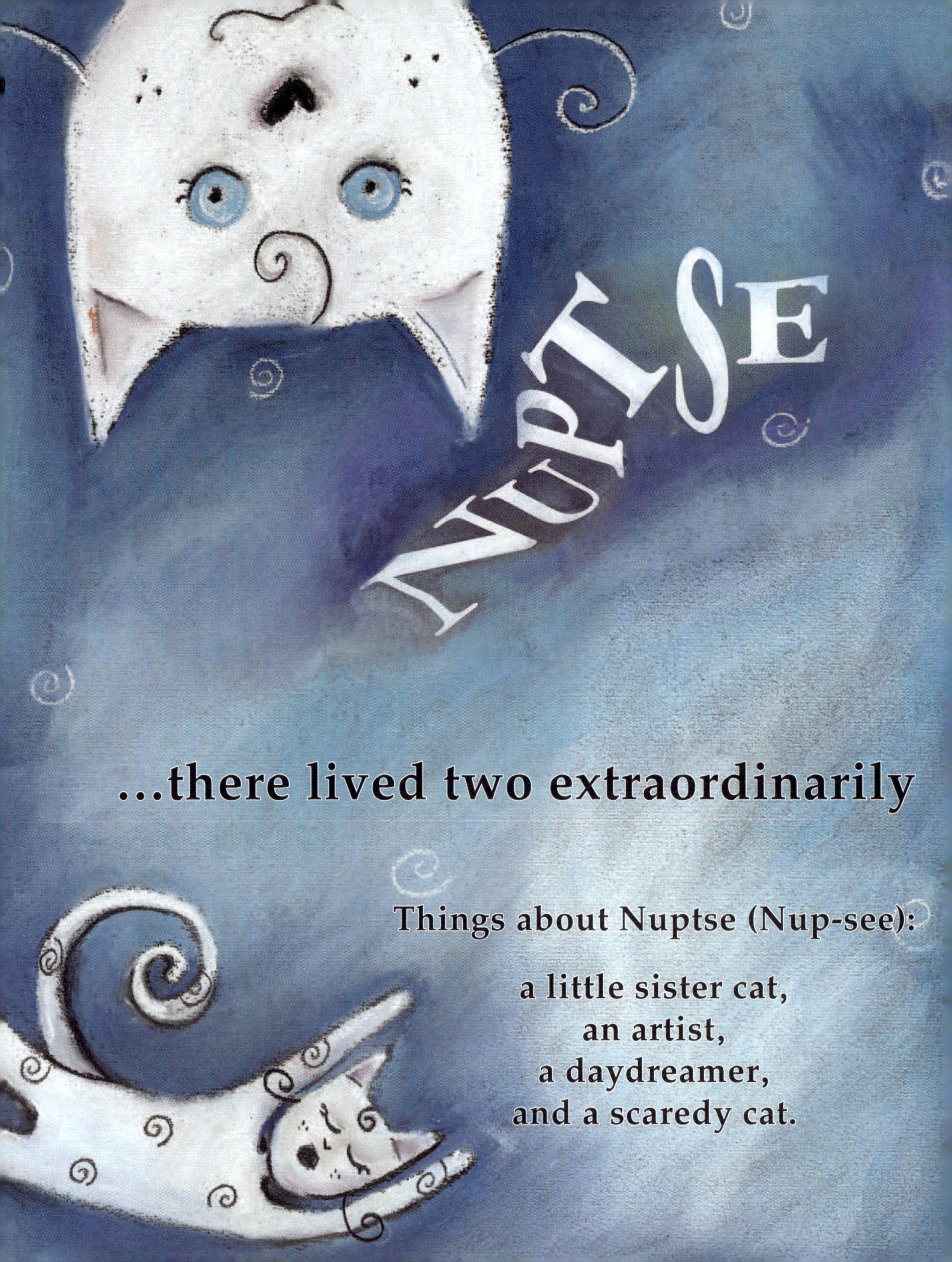

Nuptse

...there lived two extraordinarily

Things about Nuptse (Nup-see):

a little sister cat,
an artist,
a daydreamer,
and a scaredy cat.

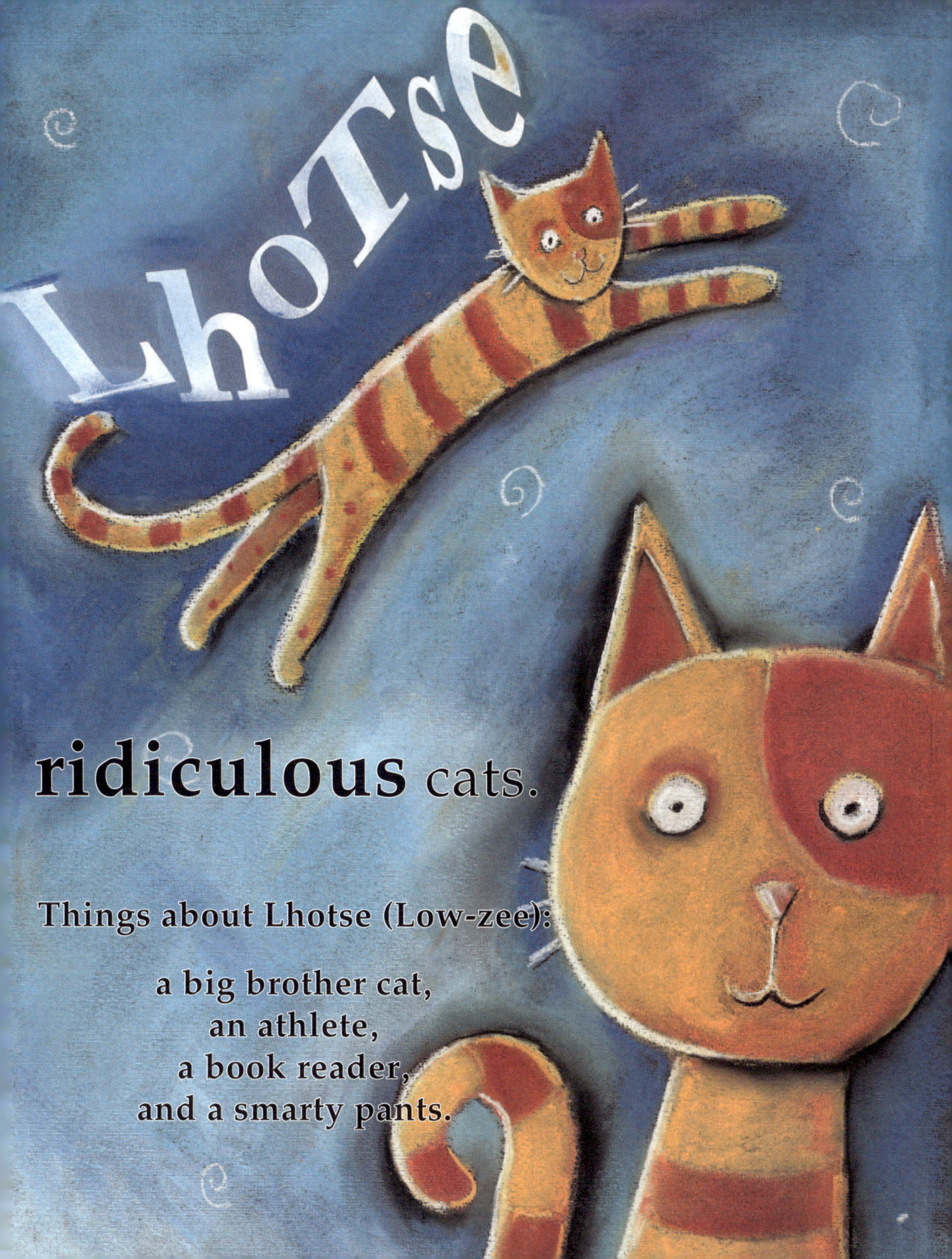

Anyways, a few minutes past the time that it was at that particular moment, Nuptse and Lhotse were behind the upside down clock looking for Nuptse's lost marbles.

"Look what I found!" said Lhotse. "It's an old map of a place called Mount Everest." He leaned over the dusty map. Nuptse began pointing excitedly at some words on the map, and then she immediately sneezed six times.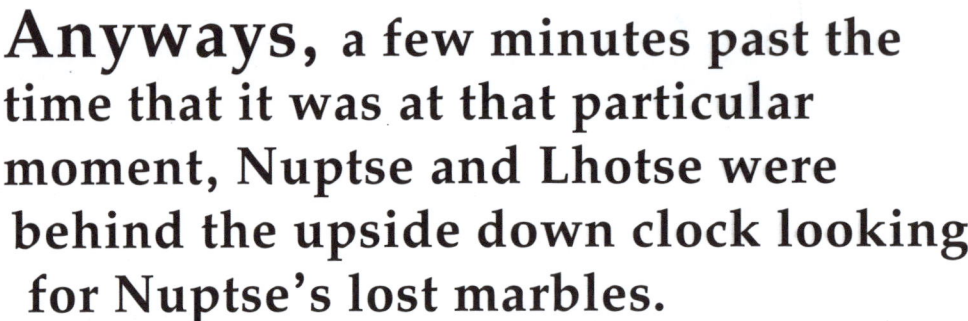

"Our NAMES are on here!" she exclaimed. "There's a Mount Nuptse and a Mount Lhotse right beside Mount Everest!"

"It looks like our mountains are in between these two lands, Nepal and Tibet," said Lhotse.

"Oh, Lhotse, we absolutely HAVE to go see our mountains right away!" said Nuptse.

So, faster than you can say Mount Everest backwards, they packed their things and chased each other outside to Lhotse's purring airplane.

"Did you know that Mount Everest is the tallest mountain in the world?" yelled Lhotse as they flew through the clouds. "Our mountains hug Mount Everest on each side. Isn't that fascinating, Nuptse? Nuptse! Are you even listening to me? What are you doing back there?"

"I wonder what colours our mountains will be," said Nuptse dreamily. "Mine will be purple, or red, no, definitely purple, I think. Or baby blue, my favourite colour! Oh, I do hope my Mount Nuptse is baby blue!"

37 seconds to fly to Nepal," said Lhotse.

Quietly, Nuptse sang to herself, "Cat-man-doo, cat-man-doo, we like you, cat-man-doo," as she followed Lhotse out of the city and into the hills.

and up and down through the hills and into the mountains.

"Nuptse, it says here on our map that we are now in the village of Lukla. The trail to our mountains will be steep, with yaks and suspension bridges and..."

"JELLYBEANS!" shouted Nuptse.

"Jellybeans? What are you talking about, Nuptse? You can't just say that the trail is full of jellybeans. It doesn't make any sense."

"Then how do you explain this?" Nuptse popped a green jellybean into her mouth and grinned. She had the funny look she got when she was keeping a secret.

"Where did you find that?" asked Lhotse. He looked at her curiously. "Wait, what's in your backpack, Nuptse?"

"Um, just some stuff for climbing mountains." Nuptse shrugged.

"Your pack is FULL of jellybeans, Nuptse!"

"I know. It's… it's all I brought," said Nuptse. "I eat them every time I feel scared."

•What should be in a backpack•
WARM jacket
WARM Hat
mittens
underwears
Long johns
first Aid
water & filter
socks
sleeping bag
toothbrush stuff
•What absolutely should never be in a backpack•
T.V.
catnip Mice
grand piano
dress-up boots
Angry bees
heavy weights

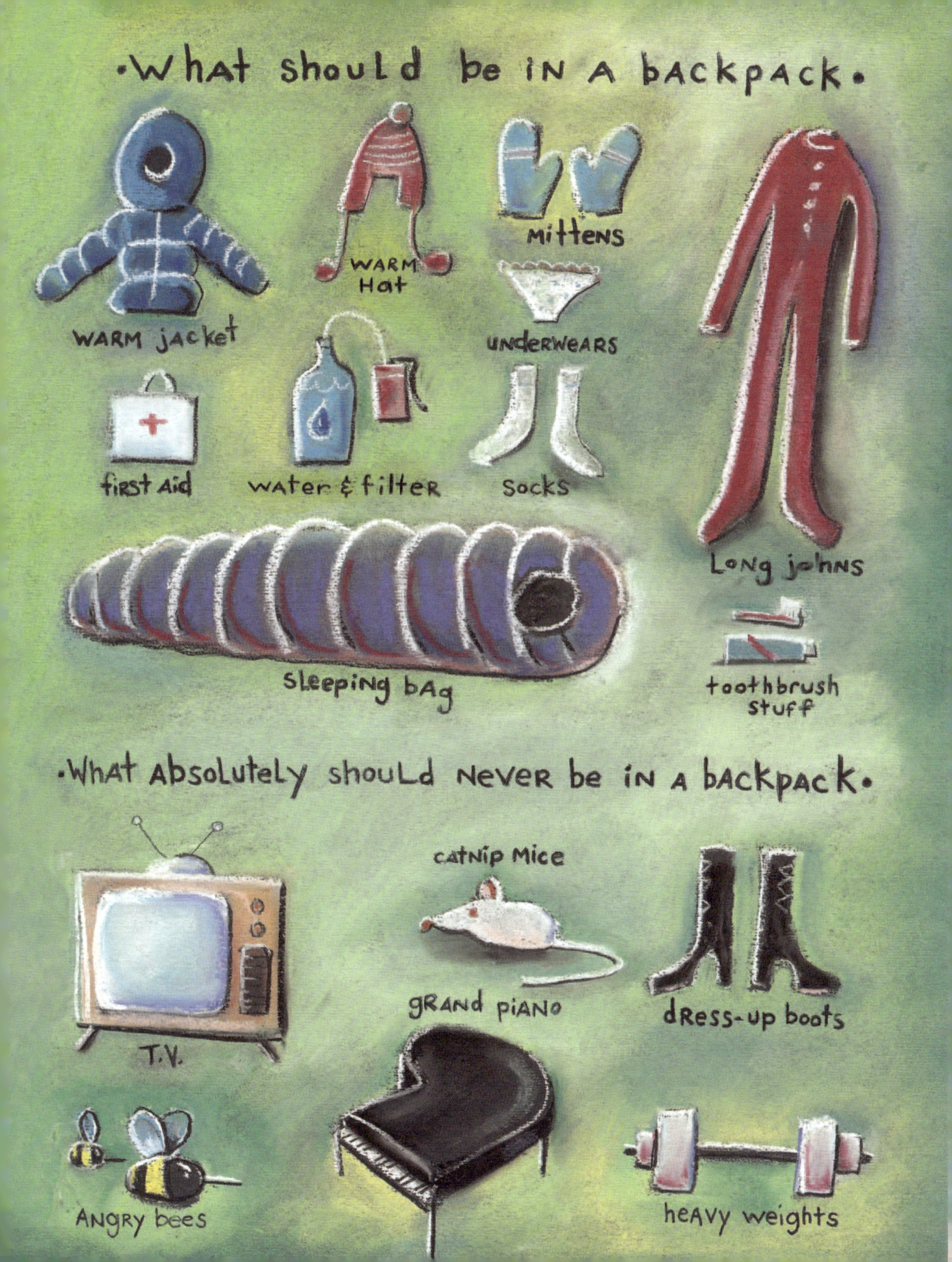

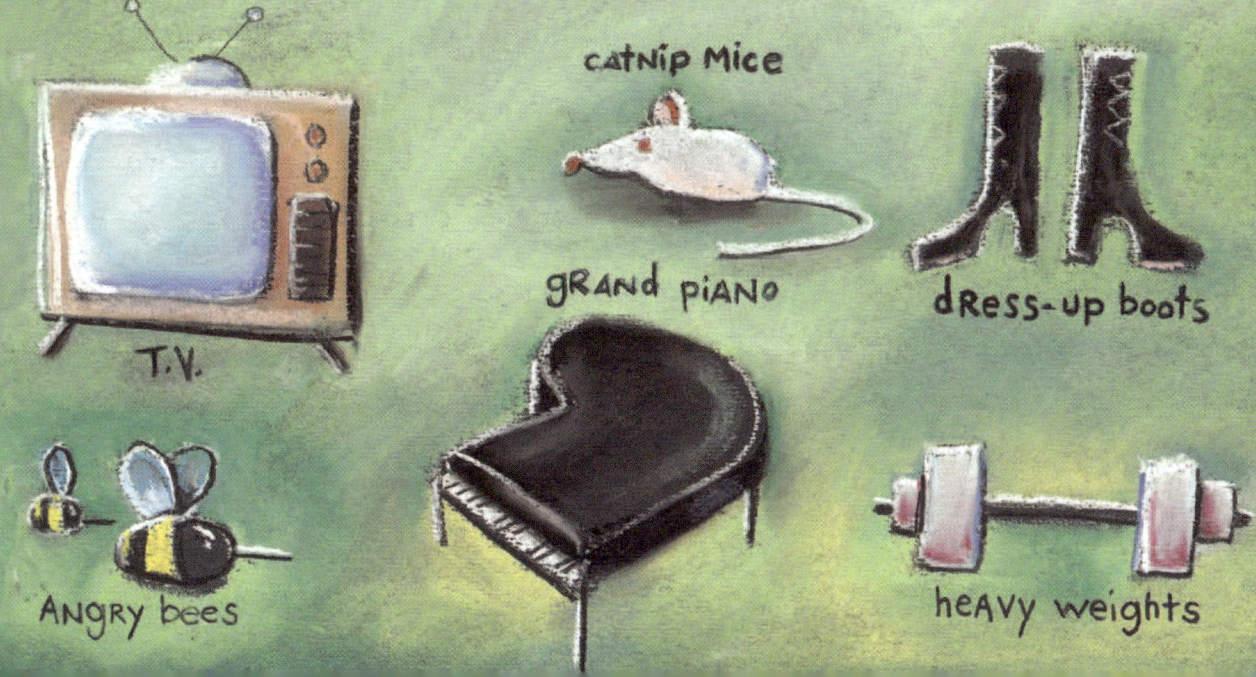

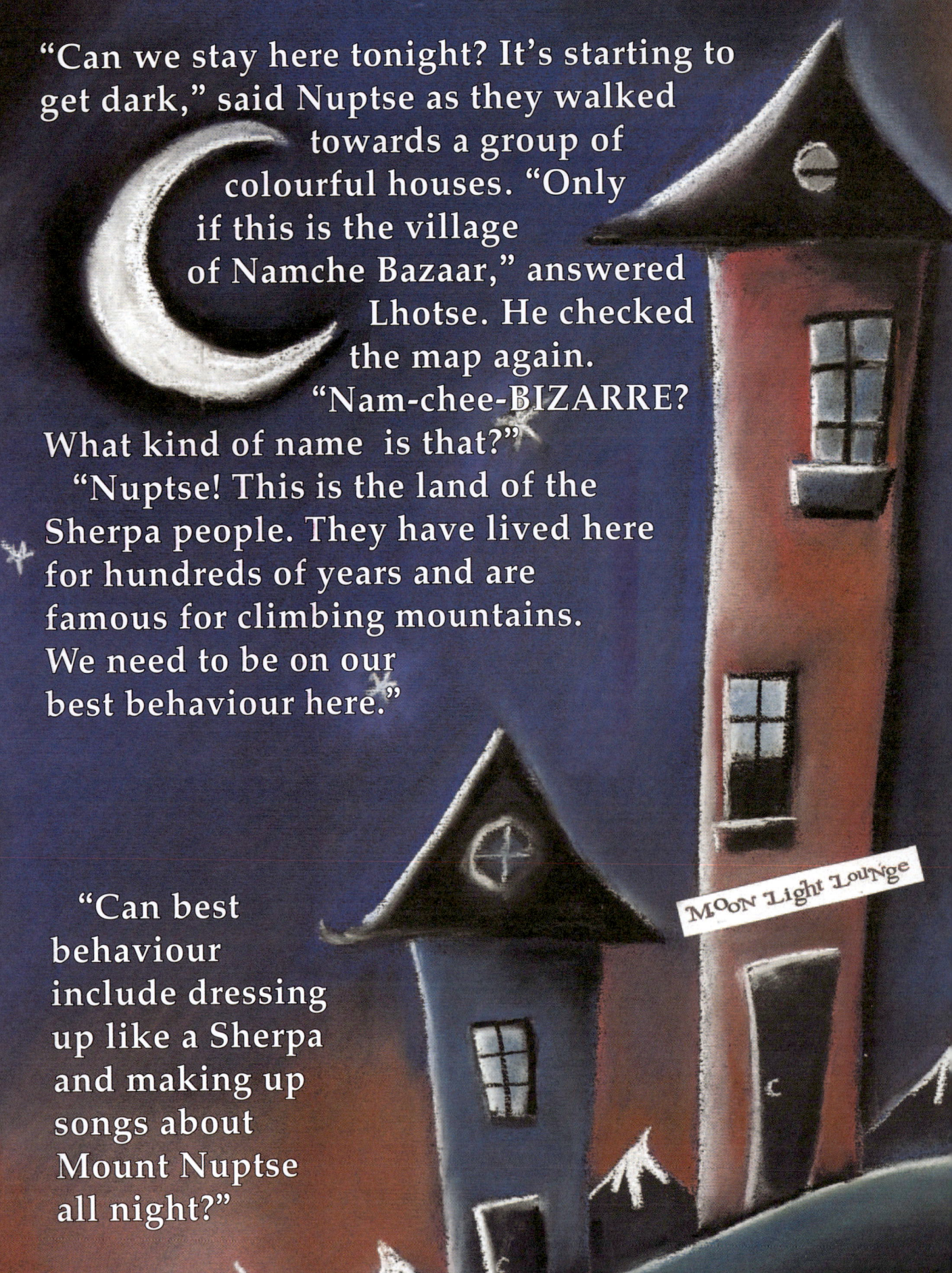

"Can we stay here tonight? It's starting to get dark," said Nuptse as they walked towards a group of colourful houses. "Only if this is the village of Namche Bazaar," answered Lhotse. He checked the map again. "Nam-chee-BIZARRE? What kind of name is that?"

"Nuptse! This is the land of the Sherpa people. They have lived here for hundreds of years and are famous for climbing mountains. We need to be on our best behaviour here."

"Can best behaviour include dressing up like a Sherpa and making up songs about Mount Nuptse all night?"

The Sun was just saying good morning to the sleepy Moon when the cats woke up the next day.

"Guess what, Nuptse? We are **higher** than anywhere we have **ever** been, and we still have to go **farther** up and then **up again.** To help us breathe, we need to take lots of catnaps so our hearts and lungs can get **stronger** in the thin air."

"What does mountain sickness feel like?" asked Nuptse.

"You get giggly, dizzy, tummy achy, and forgetful," answered Lhotse.

"And would it also make me want to walk around in circles until I fall down?"

"Yes, but Nuptse, you feel like doing that every day! You do not have **mountain sickness.**"

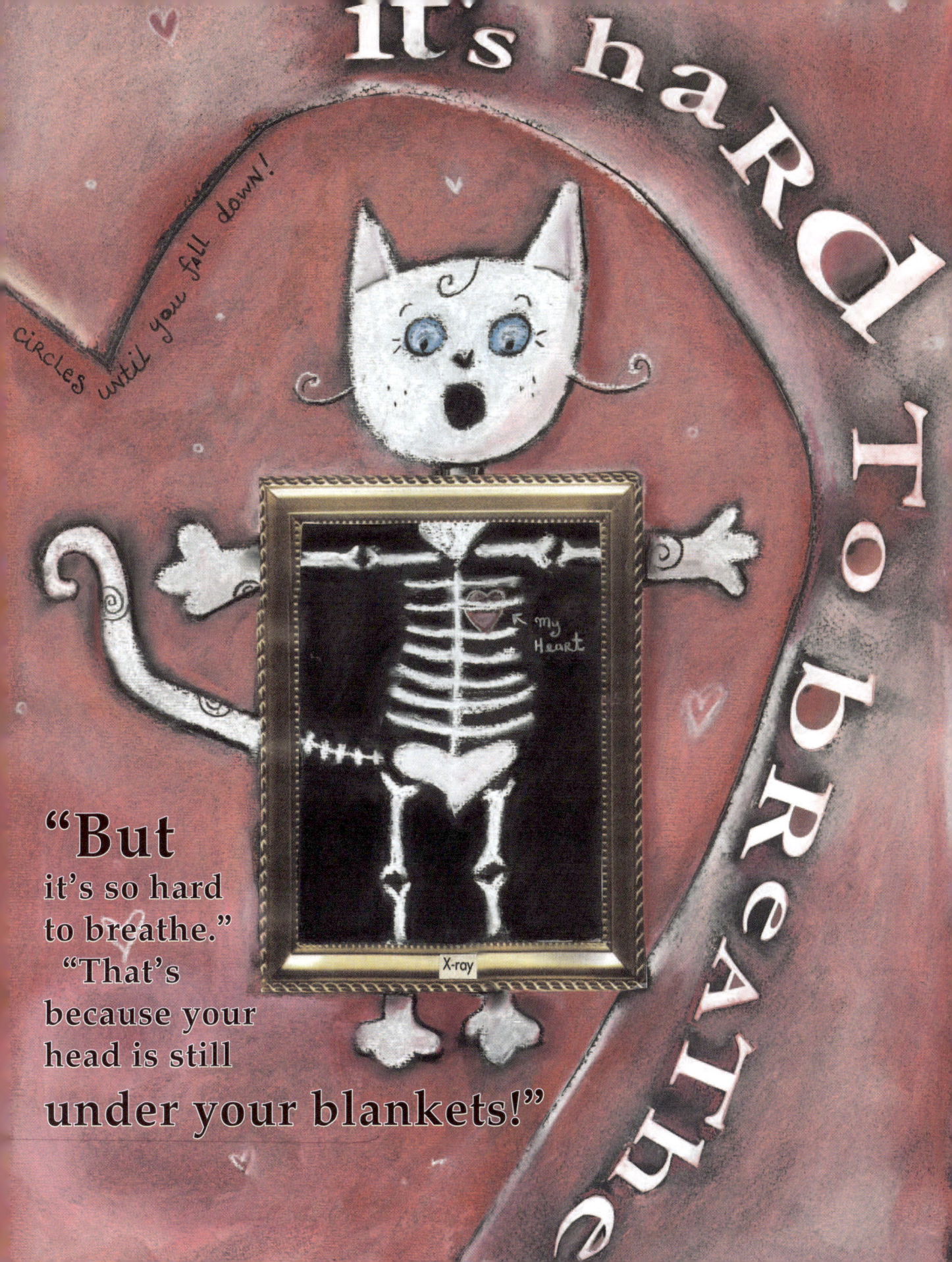

A little while later, some time the next day, the cats had to cross a high wobbly wooden bridge over the Dudh Khosi River.

"That river looks hungry," whimpered Nuptse as she looked over the railing.

"Just follow me, like this." Lhotse skipped across the bridge to the other side. Nuptse carefully tiptoed across after him, but the bridge began to swing and swoop and creak and groan.

A group of yaks with food and equipment tied high on their backs were running and jumping and leaping and bouncing onto the bridge behind her.

"Run, Nuptse!"
"I-I-I can't, I'm s-s-scared!"
"You have to! Eat some of your jellybeans!"
"I...ate...them...all...already...."
"You HAVE to run! Just DON'T LOOK DOWN!"

"**Wait!** Stop telling the story for a minute," interrupted Lhotse. "Do you really want to have the yaks in our book, Nuptse? It might be too scary to read."

"We have to put this part in to show how brave I was and stopped being scared," Nuptse said.

"But you're still scared of water, the dark, strawberry jam, and your own shadow!" Lhotse laughed.

"But not yaks anymore! Now, LET'S KEEP TELLING OUR STORY."

Nuptse took a deep breath, looked at Lhotse standing safely on the other side of the bridge, and began to run. The yaks came running right behind her.

"I DID IT! I DID IT! Did you see how fast I ran, Lhotse?"

"It was amazing! I've never seen you run so fast. I don't know if I've ever even seen you run!" said Lhotse, hugging her.

"We should let you rest at the next place on our map. It's called the Tengboche Monastery."

eight lives, nine lives, one life, two lives three

seven lives

five lives, six lives

One life, two lives, three lives, four

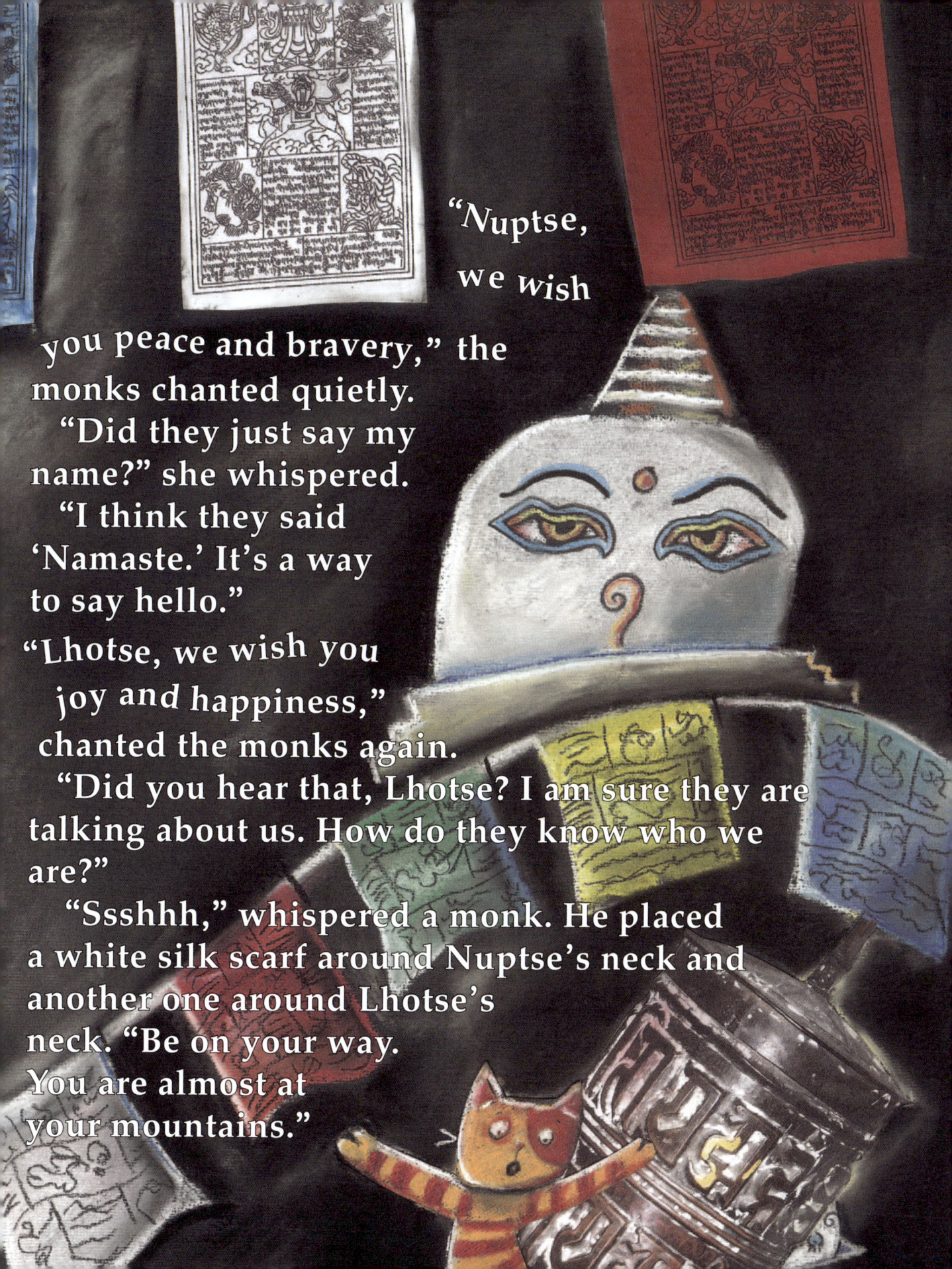

"Nuptse, we wish you peace and bravery," the monks chanted quietly.

"Did they just say my name?" she whispered.

"I think they said 'Namaste.' It's a way to say hello."

"Lhotse, we wish you joy and happiness," chanted the monks again.

"Did you hear that, Lhotse? I am sure they are talking about us. How do they know who we are?"

"Ssshhh," whispered a monk. He placed a white silk scarf around Nuptse's neck and another one around Lhotse's neck. "Be on your way. You are almost at your mountains."

It was now a day past the day that was yesterday. The cats had made it to a place called Base Camp. With frostbitten whiskers, they looked out from their tent through millions of falling snowflakes. "We need to find the Khumbu Icefall," said Lhotse, checking their map. Nuptse wandered a few feet away from him. "Does the Khumbu look like a huge frozen waterfall covered in snow?" she asked. "Yes! Can you see it?"

"It's just like walking in ice cream," yelled Nuptse. "Vanilla tuna fish sundae! Butterscotch salmon sorbet! Peppermint catnip popsicles!"

She ran up the snowy slopes, following the ropes and ladders she had found.

"Nuptse! Nuptse, wait for me! You're going the wrong way," yelled Lhotse after her.

The wind whistled his words away. He could just see the end of Nuptse's tail disappearing into the blizzard.

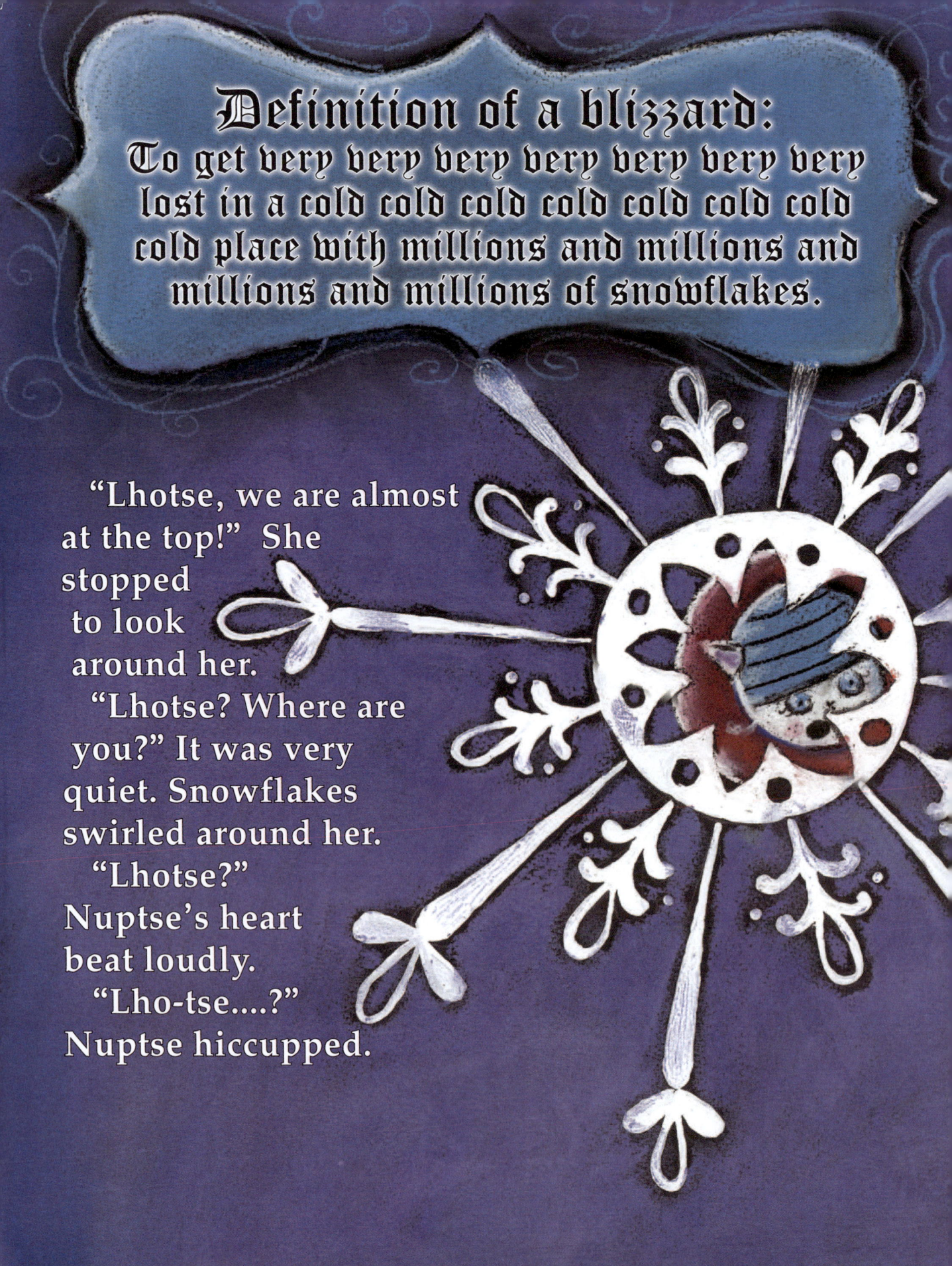

Definition of a blizzard:
To get very very very very very very very lost in a cold cold cold cold cold cold cold cold place with millions and millions and millions and millions of snowflakes.

"Lhotse, we are almost at the top!" She stopped to look around her.
"Lhotse? Where are you?" It was very quiet. Snowflakes swirled around her.
"Lhotse?" Nuptse's heart beat loudly.
"Lho-tse....?" Nuptse hiccupped.

"NUPTSE? Is that you up there?" called Lhotse out into the storm.

"LHOTSE!" Nuptse gasped. "Oh, I am so glad to see you!"

"Nuptse, I was so scared. I couldn't find you in the snowstorm and I thought I lost you forever!" said Lhotse.

"Look, we are almost at the top of

my mountain!"

"Nuptse, do you realize that we have just about climbed . . .

MOUNT

the tallest mountain

"Don't worry, Nuptse. I know

EVEREST

in the world!

"Oh no! I thought I was climbing Mount Nuptse," sniffled Nuptse. She sat in the snow and wiped a tear away with her mitten. "We've come so far, Lhotse. Will we ever get to see the mountains we were named after?"

exactly what we can do."

Nuptse and Lhotse stepped together onto Mount Everest.

"I can see the top of Mount Nuptse and Mount Lhotse from here!" said Nuptse. She danced in a tiny circle on the top of the mountain and clapped her mittens together.

"Lhotse, there are hundreds of mountains here! I want to stay here forever!"

"Look, Nuptse!" Lhotse pointed. "Don't you think our mountains kind of look like us?" Nuptse and Lhotse looked at each other and giggled.

"We did it! Do you think anyone will ever believe us?" asked Nuptse.

"I know! We'll leave our scarves and a picture of us! Then everyone who comes all the way up here will know that we did it!"

The End (almost)

"Lhotse? How do we get down from here?"

"We need to climb down."

"Climb down? Cats do NOT climb DOWN anything. I do NOT climb DOWN anything. I am NOT climbing down Mount Everest!"

"Nuptse, how do you think everyone else gets off of here?"

"I can't even think about it. Maybe I'll just stay up here."

"You can't stay up here, Nuptse. What if I told you that a Sherpa is coming to help us climb down?"

"Really? How did he know we would need help?" asked Nuptse excitedly.

"He followed us to make sure we would be safe. We'll go slowly and carefully and we'll all make it back to our homes so we can have more adventures!"

"I'll think about it. Let me just say goodbye to my mountain first."

"Finally, The End"

Lhotse's Interesting Facts

- Mount Lhotse is about 8516 m (27890 feet) high and it is the 4th highest mountain in the world.

- Mount Lhotse is taller than Mount Nuptse.

- The name for Mount Everest in Nepal is Sagarmatha. It is 8848 m (29029 feet) high and gets taller every year.

- One of the best times to CLIMB Mount Everest is in May before the monsoon rain.

- Many climbers from all over the world try each year to climb Mount Everest.

- Mount Everest can be climbed from Nepal starting near the Khumbu Icefall.

- It takes most people several weeks of training on the mountain to get to the very top of Mount Everest and get back to Base Camp.

- Sir Edmund Hillary from New Zealand and Tenzing Norgay from Nepal were the first to climb Mount Everest at 11:30 am on May 29, 1953.

- In Nepal, a porter is a person who carries heavy baskets of supplies for villages or bags and backpacks for the trekkers.

- A Yak (or Nak for females) is a mammal that looks like a big, hairy cow. They carry supplies on their backs, provide milk, butter, and cheese, and their hair can be used for wool.

- Lhotse's favourite food in Nepal was Daal Baht (rice, lentil soup, and special spices). Delicious!

Nuptse's Exciting Facts

- Mount Nuptse is about 7879 m (27755 feet) high, and is either the 19th, 20th, or 21st highest mountain in the world depending on which list you check.

- Mount Nuptse is shorter but prettier and pointier than Mount Lhotse.

- The name for Mount Everest in Tibet is Chomolungma. There is hardly any air at the top to breathe.

- One of the other best times to SEE Mount Everest is in October or November after the monsoon rain.

- Many people from all over the world come to Nepal each year just to see the highest mountains.

- Mount Everest can also be climbed from Tibet starting near the Rongbuk Glacier.

- It takes most people about 15 -18 days of trekking along dirt trails to get to see Mount Everest and get back to Kathmandu.

- George Mallory and Andrew Irvine tried to be the first to climb Mount Everest on June 8, 1924. It is a mystery whether they made it all the way to the top before they disappeared.

- In Nepal, a monk (bhikkhus) or nun (bhikkhunis) are people who have taken vows to study Buddhist wisdom and meditations. They may live in a monastery.

- A Yeti is a legend about a wandering snowman that looks like a big, hairy person. No one knows for sure if it is the truth or make-believe.

- Nuptse's favourite food in Nepal was momos (spicy dumplings) and fingerchips (fried potatoes). Yum!

A Mountain of Gratitude

It's hard for me to believe that the first edition of Nuptse and Lhotse in Nepal came out more than a decade ago, and how much has happened to these two cats since their debut.

I owe so much to those of you who were brave enough and patient enough to share the trails with me on that first trek in 2003, where this story was born, and those who have since joined me on multiple treks back to this land I love so much.

To Kiley T, for coming that first time and getting me through my scaredy-cat moments (especially on the suspension bridges). To Dave C, for sharing your fingerchips, coconut crunchies and keeping me laughing. To Neil and Joyce H, for always saying yes when I ask you to go on a trek, and helping me when I fall apart. Thank you to Buddhi, Arjun, Nawang, and Sushil, for all of your trekking support. A special mention in memory of Ramchandra S, I will always cherish how much your spirit and smile brightened every guest house, and how encouraging you were to two Canadian girls stuck for days in a Himalayan snowstorm in October 2003.

The support for Nuptse and Lhotse during its earliest drafts and since its first publication has been staggering. Thank you to Brigid B and Nicole N for reading early drafts of this story and believing in it. Thanks to the faculty and participants of the Banff Centre Writing with Style 2006 program for helping Nuptse find her voice. Thank you to all the fans of Nuptse and Lhotse from around the world! Your emails, letters and dedication to these cats and their subsequent adventures means so much to me. I am forever thankful for my family, for filling my life with mountains of stories and art supplies when I was small. To Frances K, for your friendship, all the great conversations, and your instrumental support in making this dream of a Nepal edition happen, thank you.

And always, to Jamey. For trekking by my side through it all.

A percentage of the profits from the first edition of Nuptse and Lhotse in Nepal were donated to non profit organizations that protect, support, and assist some of the most vulnerable people of Nepal. A percentage of the royalties from this edition will also be donated by the author towards supportive programs, initiatives and organizations within Nepal.

Jocey Asnong was raised by a pack of wild pencil crayons in a house made of paper and stories in a land full of maple trees. After many years of Illustration school, she moved to the mountains of Alberta, Canada, so that she could wear mittens most of the year.

When she is not shivering in a Mount Everest blizzard, she chases her cats around the 'art cave' the home studio where more stories about Nuptse and Lhotse are made.

Since her first trip to Nepal, she has returned many times over the years to the high up places she loves so much, and she can't wait to go back.

www.cautiousleroy.com

Most of this story is true,
except for the parts that are not...

In the summer of 2003, one extraordinary sleepless night would completely change the direction of my life. By 4 am, I had made the decision that I would go to Nepal in two months' time.

The moment I arrived in the Khumbu-Mount Everest region, I knew that I was in way over my head, that I was physically unprepared, and that I was definitely going to have to face some of my biggest fears. It was also extremely possible that despite how scared I was, I was already falling hopelessly in love with Nepal.

As I walked through the Himalayas those next two months, this story began to breathe within me. This story was a part of the landscape, in the songs danced around the tea house stove each night, and in the faces of the people in each village.

Returning to my home in Canada, I began longing for this country that had become such a part of me. I started illustrating and writing this story as a way to remember and to give back in some small way all that was given to me.

To the people of Nepal, Dhanyabhad (thank you).